How Do I Keep My Privacy Online?

Tricia Yearling

Online Smarts

How Do I Keep My Privacy Online?

Tricia Yearling

Enslow Publishing
101 W. 23rd Street
Suite 240
New York, NY 10011
USA

enslow.com

Words to Know

applications—Software for computers or mobile devices.

attachment—An extra part of an e-mail, such as a photo or text document, that you must click on to open.

blog—A Web site where people share thoughts and facts.

browsers—Software for navigating the resources on the Internet.

cookies—Small text files that Web browsers store on computers to keep track of information.

data—Pieces of information.

identity—The traits that make a person who he or she is.

phishing—The act of pretending to be a trustworthy place to get someone to give money.

predator—A person who tries to control or harm another person.

preferences —The choices people make about a computer's setup.

social networks—Web sites where people connect with friends and family.

spam—Unwanted email.

spyware—Software that records information about Web sites you visit on the Internet.

Contents

Privacy Is Important

The Internet is a powerful tool. You can use it to learn, play games, or watch your favorite shows. You can also use it to connect with friends or family all over the world. You can learn so much about different topics and people by using the Internet. However, if you are not careful, people can learn a lot about you too. Internet privacy is the ability to control your personal information. It is about limiting what people can learn about you online.

Why is Internet privacy important? It is important because some people use the Internet to steal from or hurt other people. You can protect yourself and your **identity** from these people. Keep your personal information, such as your name and birthday, private.

SAFETY TIP!

Mobile devices like cell phones, iPads, and laptops connect to the Internet. Be sure to keep these devices secure too.

Protect Yourself

You can protect yourself from people who want your information. Keep your personal information, such as your screen name—the name you use online—and birthday, private. If untrustworthy people cannot learn anything about you, it will be harder for them to hurt you. Making sure that your information cannot be found online is called Internet privacy.

Have a parent help you make a list of personal information so you know what to keep private.

Username and Password Safety

Your username and password allow you get into your Instagram account, read your e-mails, log on to online games, or access Web sites you sign up for. A username is one way you identify yourself online. A password is a code you create so that no one can see your information. Passwords can protect your computer so that no one else can use it. They also protect your e-mail, chats, and many Web sites. The harder a password is to guess, the safer it is.

Use your imagination when choosing a password. Make it hard for people to guess. A mix of capital and lowercase letters, symbols, and numbers can make your password one of a kind.

SAFETY TIP!

Never use your address, birthday, or phone number in your password.

If your password is "superstar," try changing it to "$up3rSt@r!" Write your passwords down and put them in a safe spot—someplace other than your backpack!

If you have a cell phone, you can lock it with a password. If you lose your phone, your phone numbers, e-mails, texts, and everything stored on your phone will be protected.

E-mail Safety

○ ○

Your e-mail can seem like your own private mailbox on the Internet. However, if you are not careful, anyone can read your messages. This can happen if someone finds out your username and password. A person who knows that information can even send e-mails pretending to be you! Change your password every few months. Delete any messages that contain private information. Do not send personal information by e-mail.

Many Web sites that you join will send you an e-mail when you sign up. These e-mails could contain information about your username. It is important to keep different passwords for every account you have. If people can access your e-mail, they can learn a lot about the different places you go online. If you use the same password on all of the sites that you join, someone could log in to all of those places as you. If you think someone is reading your e-mail, change your password right away.

Spam and Phishing

Spam messages are e-mails that offer you things you did not ask for and do not need. They can

SAFETY TIP!

Make a list of "Computer Dos and Don'ts" to hang near your computer.

Only open e-mails from people you know and trust. If an e-mail looks suspicious, just delete it.

make your e-mail send unwanted messages to other people. Delete these messages without reading them. Many e-mail programs have built-in filters that block spam and junk mail.

Identity thieves want to steal your personal information so they can buy expensive things using your name.

Phishing (FISH-ing) schemes are e-mails that use lies to trick you. They may look like e-mails from a trustworthy place, such as a bank or **social network** site. However,

SAFETY TIP!

Set up your e-mail to receive messages only from people who are in your address book.

they ask you to send personal information that can be used to steal from you. Some phishing e-mails even seem like a letter from a real person who needs your help. The person may ask you for money. Delete these e-mails immediately.

Open e-mails only from people you know and trust. If the email has an **attachment**, ask an adult before opening it. And never click on links that offer you money or prizes.

Safety in Public Places Online

If you spend time in **chat rooms**, on social networks, or have a **blog** or Web site, you need to protect your privacy. Be careful not to post or share information where just anyone can see it. Some chat rooms and Web sites may ask for information you are not supposed to share online, such as your real name and where you go to school. Sites that people pay to join may even ask you to enter your parent's credit card information. Never enter this kind of information without talking to a parent first.

Many sites have privacy policies. A privacy policy explains how a Web site might collect your information and what they do with it.

Chat rooms are fun places to talk with people. But never share your real name, address, school, or phone number with them.

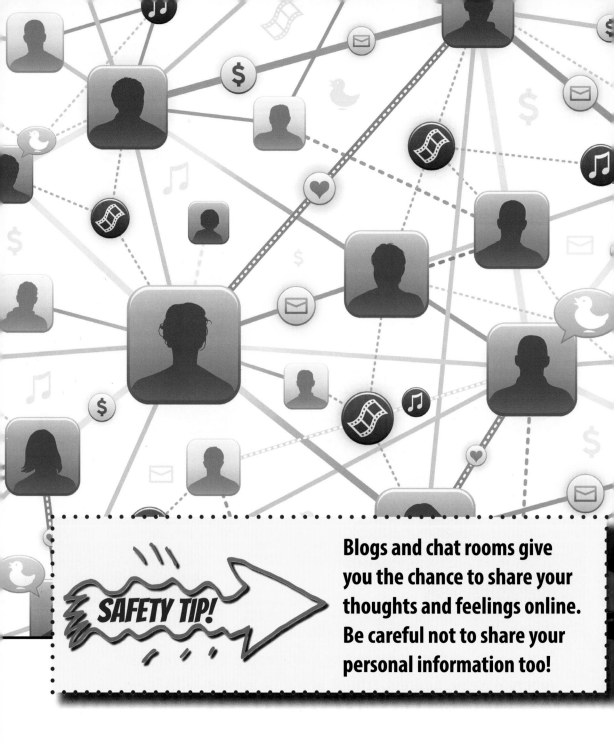

SAFETY TIP!

Blogs and chat rooms give you the chance to share your thoughts and feelings online. Be careful not to share your personal information too!

If a site requires you to give up your personal information, do not use that site. Instead, ask a teacher or librarian to help you find a site that is safe and that protects your privacy.

Spying on You

Web **browsers** leave **cookies** on your computer when you use them. Cookies are sets of information. They store passwords, settings, or other **data**. Cookies also let Web sites know what other Web sites you visit. You cannot turn off cookies. However, you can delete cookies. Settings to delete cookies can be found in your browser **preferences**. Web sites may leave cookies on school and library computers too. A teacher or librarian can show you how to get rid of these cookies.

Some sites also use software called **spyware** to track your Internet use. Companies usually use

this data to try to sell you things. Some spyware can can track the keys you type on your keyboard. Thieves use spyware to try to steal passwords. Avoid spyware by not downloading unknown **applications** to your computer. The Mac App Store or cnet.com are safe places to download software. Always talk to an adult before downloading any new apps.

Avoiding Online Predators

The Internet can be a great place to learn and have fun, but there are some people who use the Internet to harm children. These people are

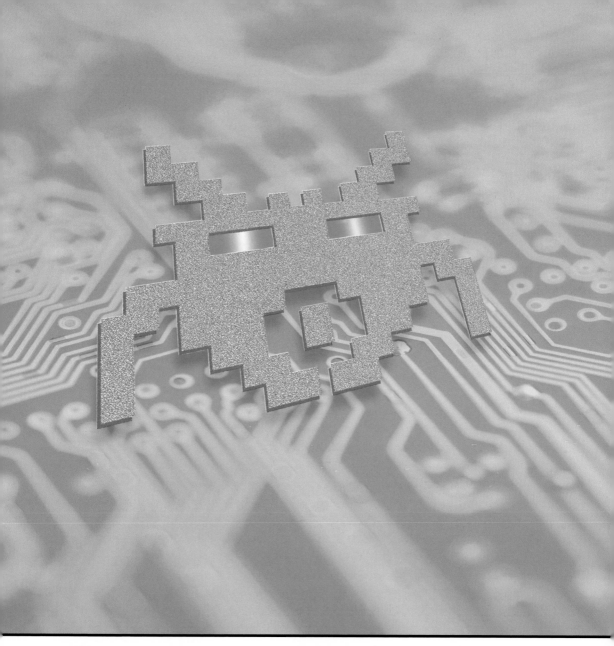

Anti-spyware programs can get rid of or block some kinds of spyware. Some programs are free. Others have to be bought.

If someone online asks to meet you in person, tell an adult right away.

known as online **predators**. Online predators may pretend to be your age to become your friend. If a stranger tries to contact you in a chat room, on a message board, or by e-mail, do not answer. If somebody asks you to send pictures of yourself or sends you pictures, tell an adult. Online predators break the law. An adult may need to call the police.

Do not let online predators make you feel guilty. The predator is the one who has done something wrong. If a predator sends you a message, it is not your fault.

The Privacy Protection Act

If you are younger than 13 years old, there is a law that protects your online privacy. The Children's Online Privacy Protection Act (COPPA) makes it illegal for Web sites to gather information about you unless your parents say it is okay. The law also lets parents track what information Web sites have gathered about their kids.

Many Web sites have age requirements to sign up. For example, users on Facebook, the largest online social network, have to be at least 13 years

Age requirements on social media sites such as Facebook are there to keep you and your personal information safe.

old. Do not use a site that you are not old enough to be on. This is for your own safety. Privacy settings on sites for adults may be complicated or confusing. You may be putting yourself and your privacy at risk by visiting these sites.

Deleting Your Data

You may discover that something has been posted about you on the Internet. The information may be there because you made a mistake and put it online. A friend may have made a bad choice and posted your photo, phone number, or e-mail address. Bullies also sometimes put other people's information online on purpose.

You may be able to delete a post or comment or ask the friend who posted it to delete the information. If it cannot be deleted, talk to an adult, such as a parent or teacher. An adult may have to contact the site to have the information taken down. Act fast and fix the problem. Do not be scared or ignore it. That information may not go away by itself. Protecting your Internet privacy is important!

SAFETY TIP!

Do not write anything about your friends online without checking with them first. Good friends protect each other's Internet privacy.

Learn More

Books

Cosson, M. J. *The Smart Kid's Guide to Using the Internet.* North Mankato, Minn.: The Child's World, 2014.

DiOrio, Rana. *What Does It Mean to Be Safe?* San Francisco, Calif.: Little Pickle Press, 2011.

Rustad, Martha E. H. *Learning About Privacy.* Mankato, Minn.: Capstone Press, 2015.

Web Sites

commonsensemedia.org/privacy-and-internet-safety

Read articles and watch videos on privacy and Internet safety.

privacy.getnetwise.org/sharing/tips/passwords

Learn tips on how to keep your passwords safe.

netsmartz.org/NetSmartzKids/PasswordRap

Watch a fun rap video on passwords!

Index

Published in 2016 by Enslow Publishing, LLC.
101 W. 23rd Street, Suite 240, New York, NY 10011

Library of Congress Cataloging-in-Publication Data
Library of Congress Cataloging-in-Publication Data
Yearling, Tricia.
 How do I keep my privacy online? / Tricia Yearling.
    pages cm. — (Online smarts)
 Includes bibliographical references and index.
 Summary: "Discusses how kids can create safe passwords and what kind of information should never be posted online"—
Provided by publisher.
 Audience: 8-up.
 Audience: Grade 4 to 6.
 ISBN 978-0-7660-6843-8 (library binding)
 ISBN 978-0-7660-6841-4 (pbk.)
 ISBN 978-0-7660-6842-1 (6-pack)
 1. Computer networks—Security measures—Juvenile literature. 2. Internet—Security measures—Juvenile literature.
 I. Title.
 TK5105.59.Y445 2015
 005.8—dc23   2015007004

Printed in the United States of America

To Our Readers: We have done our best to make sure all Web sites in this book were active and appropriate when we went to press. However, the author and the publisher have no control over and assume no liability for the material available on those Web sites or on any Web sites they may link to. Any comments or suggestions can be sent by e-mail to customerservice@ enslow.com.